Chinese New Year

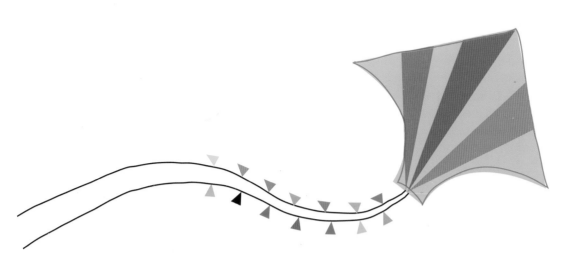

LABURNUM
PRESS

Katie Dicker

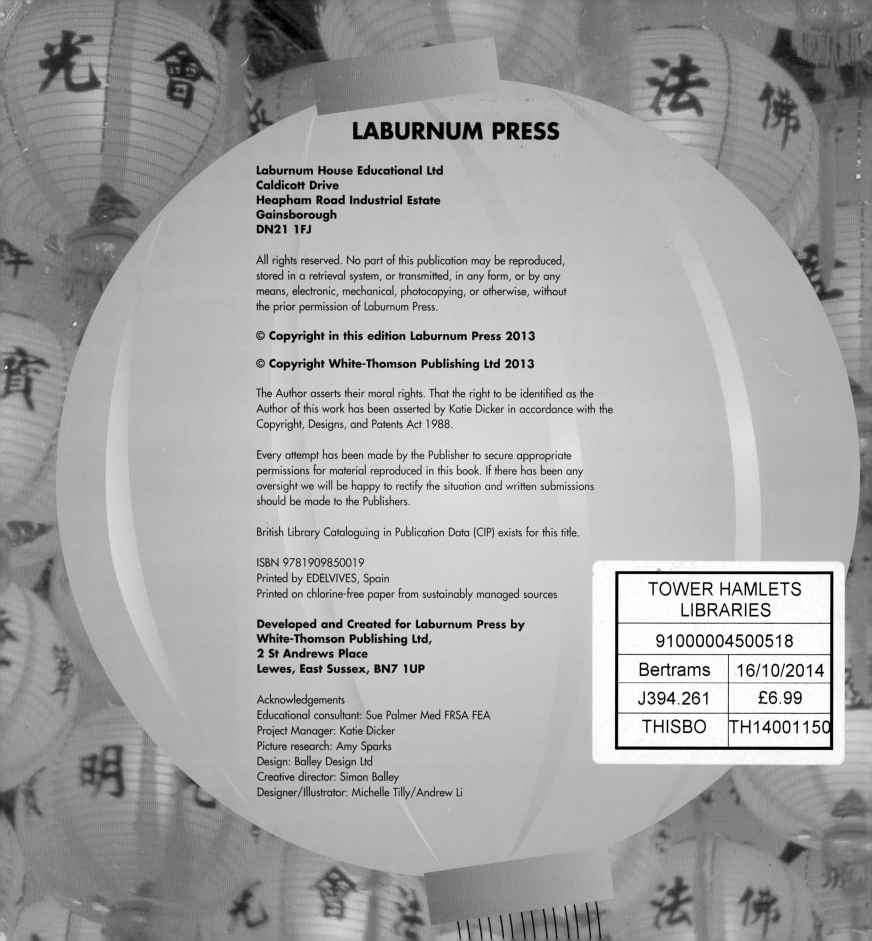

LABURNUM PRESS

Laburnum House Educational Ltd
Caldicott Drive
Heapham Road Industrial Estate
Gainsborough
DN21 1FJ

British Library Cataloguing in Publication Data (CIP) exists for this title.

ISBN 9781909850019
Printed by EDELVIVES, Spain
Printed on chlorine-free paper from sustainably managed sources

Developed and Created for Laburnum Press by
White-Thomson Publishing Ltd,
2 St Andrews Place
Lewes, East Sussex, BN7 1UP

Acknowledgements
Educational consultant: Sue Palmer Med FRSA FEA
Project Manager: Katie Dicker
Picture research: Amy Sparks
Design: Balley Design Ltd
Creative director: Simon Balley
Designer/Illustrator: Michelle Tilly/Andrew Li

Contents

Our celebrations last for fifteen days.

At the end, we'll see a full moon.

glow

Then we decorate our homes.

This fish will bring us good fortune.

scales

7

Paper patterns

That was tricky!

What animal shapes can YOU cut out?

8

Family feast

chopsticks

On New Year's eve, we share a big meal with our family.

We LOVE dumplings! How many can YOU see in each pot?

Giving gifts

oranges

The next day, we give gifts

to our family and friends.

What would YOU do with the money inside a red packet?

Up in the air!

swoosh!

On the last day of our celebrations, we fly lucky kites.

We hang paper lanterns in the dark.

They help to make the future bright.

15

Dragon dance

s-t-r-e-t-c-h!

A dragon dance frightens away evil spirits.

Grrrr!

What would YOU use to make a big monster?

17

City celebrations

In New York, there's a special parade at Chinese New Year.

flutter

In London, coloured flags and lanterns fill the streets.

19

The Chinese calendar

The Chinese years are named after 12 animals. What are they?

What animal year were YOU born in?

Notes for adults

Sparklers books are designed to support and extend the learning of young children. The **Food We Eat** titles won a Practical Pre-School Silver Award, the **Body Moves** titles won a Practical Pre-School Gold Award and the **Out and About** titles won the 2009 Practical Pre-School Gold Overall Winner Award. The books' high-interest subjects link in to the Early Years curriculum and beyond. Find out more about Early Years and reading with children from the National Literacy Trust (www.literacytrust.org.uk).

Themed titles

Chinese New Year is one of four **Celebrations** titles that encourage children to learn about annual festivals and different cultures around the world. The other titles are:

Christmas   **Easter**   **Divali**

Areas of learning

Each **Celebrations** title helps to support the following Early Years Foundation Stage areas of learning:
Personal, Social and Emotional Development
Communication, Language and Literacy
Problem Solving, Reasoning and Numeracy
Knowledge and Understanding of the World
Physical Development
Creative Development

Making the most of reading time

When reading with younger children, take time to explore the pictures together. Ask children to find, identify, count or describe different objects. Point out colours and textures. Allow quiet spaces in your reading so that children can ask questions or repeat your words. Try pausing mid-sentence so that children can predict the next word. This sort of participation develops early reading skills.

Follow the words with your finger as you read. The main text is in Infant Sassoon, a clear, friendly font designed for children learning to read and write. The labels and sound effects add fun and give the opportunity to distinguish between levels of communication. Where appropriate, labels, sound effects or main text may be presented phonically. Encourage children to imitate the sounds.

As you read the book, you can also take the opportunity to talk about the book itself with appropriate vocabulary such as "page", "cover", "back", "front", "photograph", "label" and "page number".

You can also extend children's learning by using the books as a springboard for discussion and further activities. There are a few suggestions on the facing page. The Internet also has many teaching resources about annual festivals. For example, see www.365celebration.com and www.underfives.co.uk.

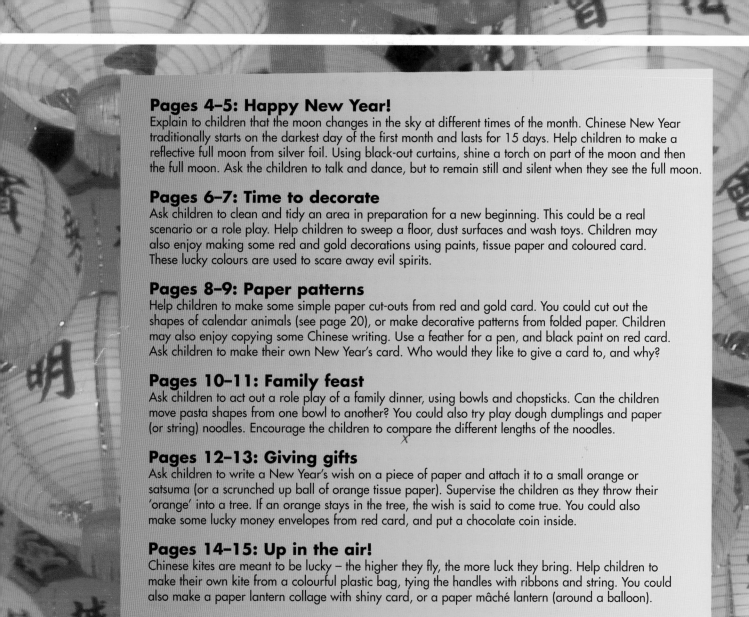

Pages 4–5: Happy New Year!

Explain to children that the moon changes in the sky at different times of the month. Chinese New Year traditionally starts on the darkest day of the first month and lasts for 15 days. Help children to make a reflective full moon from silver foil. Using black-out curtains, shine a torch on part of the moon and then the full moon. Ask the children to talk and dance, but to remain still and silent when they see the full moon.

Pages 6–7: Time to decorate

Ask children to clean and tidy an area in preparation for a new beginning. This could be a real scenario or a role play. Help children to sweep a floor, dust surfaces and wash toys. Children may also enjoy making some red and gold decorations using paints, tissue paper and coloured card. These lucky colours are used to scare away evil spirits.

Pages 8–9: Paper patterns

Help children to make some simple paper cut-outs from red and gold card. You could cut out the shapes of calendar animals (see page 20), or make decorative patterns from folded paper. Children may also enjoy copying some Chinese writing. Use a feather for a pen, and black paint on red card. Ask children to make their own New Year's card. Who would they like to give a card to, and why?

Pages 10–11: Family feast

Ask children to act out a role play of a family dinner, using bowls and chopsticks. Can the children move pasta shapes from one bowl to another? You could also try play dough dumplings and paper (or string) noodles. Encourage the children to compare the different lengths of the noodles.

Pages 12–13: Giving gifts

Ask children to write a New Year's wish on a piece of paper and attach it to a small orange or satsuma (or a scrunched up ball of orange tissue paper). Supervise the children as they throw their 'orange' into a tree. If an orange stays in the tree, the wish is said to come true. You could also make some lucky money envelopes from red card, and put a chocolate coin inside.

Pages 14–15: Up in the air!

Chinese kites are meant to be lucky – the higher they fly, the more luck they bring. Help children to make their own kite from a colourful plastic bag, tying the handles with ribbons and string. You could also make a paper lantern collage with shiny card, or a paper mâché lantern (around a balloon).

Pages 16–17: Dragon dance

Help children to put on their own dragon dance, using masks or a dragon puppet. You could make a small dragon (using sticks attached to concertina paper), or a larger dragon with a cardboard box head and a material body. Encourage the children to make their own music for the dance, with drums, cymbals or other loud sounds. The loudest noises frighten the bad spirits away.

Pages 18–19: City celebrations

Help children to put on their own New Year parade. Ask them to wear an item of red clothing, or to make their own red hats. You could also make some coloured bunting to add to the festival atmosphere.

Pages 20–21: The Chinese calendar

Talk to children about the stories behind the Chinese calendar. Use the Internet to help you (see www.topmarks.co.uk/chinesenewyear/zodiacstory.aspx, for example). Explain the different characteristics of each animal. Can the children act them out? Children may also enjoy making their own animal masks or costumes for their role play.

Index

Picture acknowledgements:
Alamy: 19 (Mark Baynes); **Corbis:** cover (Inmagine Asia), 8 (Yi Lu), 9 (Imagemore Co., Ltd.), 13 (Yang Liu), 16 (So Hing-Keung), 17 (Inmagine Asia); **Dreamstime:** 4 (Serguei Bachlakov), 5 (confidential info); **Getty Images:** 10 (Lane Oatey), 18 (Roy Kemp and Russell Knight), 21 (Andy Crawford and Dave King); **Istockphoto:** 20 (Ace Create); **Photolibrary:** 6 (Blue Jean Images LLC), 7 (Blue Jean Images LLC), 12 (Asia Selects), 14 (Blue Jean Images LLC); **Shutterstock:** cover fireworks (Gilmanshin), 2-3 lanterns (Photobank), 9 inset (Ho Yeow Hui), 11 (immanuel001), 15 (Norman Chan), 22-23 lanterns (Photobank), 24 lanterns (Photobank).